D0590555

700023579912

A Young Citizen's Guide To:

Political Parties

Pat Levy

W
HODDER
Wayland
An imprint of Hodder Children's Books

A Young Citizen's Guide series

Central Government
Local Government
Money
Parliament
Political Parties
The Criminal Justice System
The Electoral System
The European Union
The Media in Politics
Voluntary Groups

© Copyright 2002 Hodder Wayland

Published in Great Britain in 2002 by Hodder Wayland,
an imprint of Hodder Children's Books

Editor: Patience Coster
Design: Simon Borrough
Picture research: Glass Onion Pictures
Artwork: Stefan Chabluk
Consultant: Dr Stephen Coleman

British Library Cataloguing in Publication Data
Levy, Patricia, 1951-
A young citizen's guide to political parties
1. Political parties - Great Britain - Juvenile literature
2. Great Britain - politics and government - 1997- -
Juvenile literature I. Title II. Political parties
324.2'41

ISBN 0 7502 4090 3

Printed and bound in Hong Kong

Hodder Children's Books,
a division of Hodder Headline
Limited, 338 Euston Road,
London NW1 3BH

Picture acknowledgements:
the publisher would like to
thank the following for
permission to use their
pictures: Mary Evans Picture
Library 10, 11; PA Photos 13;
Photofusion 7 (bottom, Ray
Roberts), 8 (Robert Brook),
24 (Bob Watkins), 25 (Libby
Welch), 26 (Graham Burns),
28 (Don Gray), 29 (Libby
Welch); Popperfoto/Reuters 6
(Dan Chung), 14 (Jeff Mitchell),
23 (Sean Dempsey); Topham/
Associated Press 18; Topham
Picturepoint 17, 20 (top);
Topham/Press Association 5
(Sean Dempsey), 9 (John
Stillwell), 16 (Phil Noble), 19
(Andrew Parsons), 20 (bottom)
and contents page (Andrew
Parsons), 22 (Stefan
Rousseau), 27; Topham/
Pressnet 4 and title page
(Tasha Mottram), 7 (top,
Jeff Moore).

Cover: Conservative Central
Office (Photofusion/Paul Doyle);
Labour Party conference
(Topham/Chris Ison); Liberal
Democrat leader Charles
Kennedy (Popperfoto/
Dan Chung).

Contents

What are Political Parties?   4

The Origins of Political Parties   10

How Political Parties are Managed   15

People in Political Parties   24

You and Political Parties   28

Glossary   30

Resources   31

Index   32

Political parties in the UK are organizations that represent the different political views of the citizens, putting forward sets of ideas for governing the country. In a general election, political parties put forward candidates for election to Parliament. Each candidate hopes to represent a particular area of the UK; these areas are known as constituencies. All citizens over the age of eighteen are invited to vote for the candidate they prefer. The winning candidate in each constituency becomes an MP (Member of Parliament) and sits in the House of Commons, which is where new laws and issues are discussed and voted upon. General elections must take place at least once every five years.

Forming a government
The political party with the largest number of MPs forms the government of the country. If the governing party has more MPs than all the other parties put together, it has what is called an overall majority. In 1924, 1974 and 1977 the Labour Party failed to win an overall majority and held power with the co-operation of a third party, the Liberals.

Labour Party candidate Andy Slaughter campaigns in a bye-election in July 1997.

The leader of the governing party is the Prime Minister, and he or she governs with the advice of the Cabinet. This is a group of MPs who are government ministers and belong to the governing party. At election times, most UK citizens vote for a party rather than an individual MP, and the party that wins the largest number of seats in Parliament wins the election and so forms the Cabinet.

Parliament makes laws by a vote of all MPs, who in most cases vote as their party tells them. The laws they make are chosen mainly by the Cabinet. So either through the government of the Cabinet or through MPs voting laws into place, the party that wins the general election with an overall majority usually has control over the running of the country. This process is known as parliamentary democracy. The only way a government's decisions can be defeated in Parliament is by a rebellion of a sizeable number of MPs.

Since the outcome of each election is uncertain, all parties with a chance of winning form a government in waiting, with nominated Cabinet members and a potential Prime Minister. The idea is that there is always a second government ready to come to power. The leader of the Opposition (the party with the next largest number of MPs) receives a salary from the government.

'The party system, although necessary, is not the be-all and end-all of a live democracy.
I believe that there is a need for more Independents at both the local and national level. They consider every issue on its merits. They speak with a distinctive voice. They provide a corrective to the occasional failures of party politics.'
Martin Bell, Independent MP, speaking in 2001.

The current Prime Minister, Tony Blair (blue shirt, centre left) with his Cabinet in June 2001.

A wasted vote?
Non-party, or Independent, MPs are very rare. In the last two parliaments there have been two Independent MPs. So why do people take the trouble to go to the polling station and waste their votes on someone who has little chance of being elected, or fulfilling his or her election promises even if they were elected? Many people choose to vote on single or local issues, such as motorway building or joining the single European currency, because they feel very strongly about that particular subject. For the most part, these candidates never win, but in 1997 Independent candidate Martin Bell was famously elected on an anti-sleaze platform after most of the other candidates withdrew, leaving a contest between Bell and the Conservative candidate, Neil Hamilton.

What political parties do In the UK, the political parties perform the following functions. They:

- recruit politicians. All politicians start out as members of their local political party. If a politician is able to impress other party members that he or she can win people's votes and do a good job as a local council member, party official or candidate for Parliament, then the local party nominates him or her for office.
- develop policies to present to the country. Even small parties such as the Green Party, which has little hope of being elected to government, produce manifestos outlining their ideas.
- organize election campaigns.
- provide political choices for voters. In their election manifestos, the parties offer the electorate a package of policies, which generally covers a wide range of beliefs and opinions on how to run the country. From these packages, voters choose the party they think most corresponds to their views.
- allow people to take part in the political process. By joining a party, a person has an opportunity to influence the selection of his or her MP and to decide what the party's policies are to be. However, the number of people who take an active part in the political process by joining a local party is very low and decreases each year.
- generate political argument and information. Because elections have become so closely linked to parties rather than to individual candidates, electioneering rarely stops.

Posting a ballot paper into a sealed ballot box at an election. When voting is finished, the boxes are taken to a centre where the votes are counted.

6

Senior members of the Labour government get together to launch the party manifesto for the 2001 general election.

To maintain a high and favourable profile with the voting public, the party in power regularly issues policy initiatives (new ideas on how to run the country) or makes surveys on improvements within the public services, such as the National Health Service (NHS) or police. The Opposition finds ways to criticize government policy. It draws attention to government failures and suggests better methods of dealing with issues.

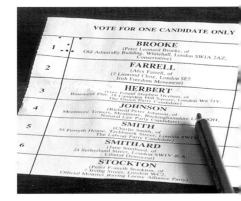

- maintain the system of government and opposition. Once the election is over, the party in power takes charge of the business of government. The governing party decides the agenda for each parliament and the Opposition provides a dissenting voice.

A ballot paper. Although voting is by secret ballot, each paper has a reference number so that the voter can be traced if necessary.

Britain's political parties There are three main political parties in the UK, the Labour Party, the Conservative Party and the Liberal Democrat Party. They have different views about major issues, such as the following:

Public spending The Labour Party believes in a partnership between public bodies and private industries to improve health care, prisons, schools and other previously publicly funded bodies. The Conservative Party is committed to tight control of public spending and favours the privatization of many publicly funded and run organizations, such as the NHS, the London Underground and air traffic control. The Liberal Democrats believe in keeping these services in the public sector.

Taxation While the Labour Party has traditionally been in favour of increasing taxes, the Conservative Party has generally been in favour of lowering them. However, in the last ten years the Labour Party has tried not to raise taxes because it is an unpopular policy with most voters. Critics have accused the Labour Party of introducing 'stealth taxes', in other words putting indirect taxes on goods rather than raising income tax. The Liberal Democrat Party believes that taxation should be increased very slightly to pay for welfare improvements.

Education The Labour Party believes in investing in the state education system, but it also encourages the development of independent schools. The Conservative Party believes that all schools should be able to select some of their pupils. The Liberal Democrats say that they would increase taxation to raise an annual £3 billion for schools and colleges.

Posters for the three main parties appeal to voters in the run-up to a general election.

Voting system The Liberal Democrats believe in the introduction of proportional representation (PR) as the voting system in the UK. PR means that MPs would be elected on the proportion of votes their party gets nationally instead of by the 'first-past-the-post' system that operates at the moment. With the 'first-past-the-post' system, the person with the most votes in each constituency wins the election, and no account is taken of the wishes of all the people who voted for their opponents. For example, in 1992 more UK citizens voted for the Labour Party than the Conservative Party, but the Conservative Party won more seats, so it formed the government.

As well as the three main parties, there are several smaller parties which tend to focus on single issues.

- The Green Party stresses the importance of environmental protection. It has lost much national support since the major parties have all taken up aspects of its ideas, such as the control of pollution or recycling domestic rubbish.
- The Scottish National Party (SNP) and Welsh Plaid Cymru focus on independence for their countries. Both supported the move to devolve local governments for Scotland and Wales.
- Parties that focus on the politics of Northern Ireland include the Ulster Unionists, Democratic Unionist Party, the Progressive Unionist Party, the Social Democratic and Labour Party (SDLP) and Sinn Fein.

Political parties often elicit support from celebrities to draw attention to their cause. Here Penny Kemp, chairperson of the Green Party, is pictured outside the Houses of Parliament with model and actress Bianca Jagger.

9

Political groups existed in Britain long before there was an electorate to vote for them. For centuries, rival groups of noblemen fought for the patronage of the monarch. In the late seventeenth century, the terms 'Tory' and 'Whig' began to be used to describe two distinct political attitudes. The former supported the power of the monarch, the latter tried to restrict the monarch's power in favour of wealthy, land-owning lords. In the eighteenth century, MPs were landowners who voted according to their own interests and often clubbed together to get a bill passed into law. Each MP considered himself either a Whig or a Tory, but there were no formal parties.

Until 1832, only 435,000 men in Britain had the vote, and most of them lived in rural areas. Candidates for Parliament did little in the way of electioneering, instead they bribed voters with beer or cash. Huge inequalities existed: for example, cities such as Manchester and Birmingham had no MPs, whereas Cornwall, which had a very small population, sent 44 representatives to Parliament. In some areas, known as 'rotten boroughs', there were no voters at all and the local landowner simply chose who would be the MP. Instead of a secret ballot, where people cast their votes in private, votes were counted from a show of hands.

This cartoon shows a gentleman being paid off after registering his vote. Such practices were commonplace before the introduction of the secret ballot.

The Reform Act
In 1832, Parliament passed a Reform Act. This gave the vote to thousands more men, many of whom had moved from the

countryside to work in the fast-growing towns and cities. Women and working-class men without property, however, were still not entitled to vote. Further electoral reforms in the nineteenth century extended the vote to a million more men, and soon voters were aligning themselves with organized political parties. After 1815, the Whig Party was renamed the Liberal Party, and the Liberals and Tories (Conservatives) began to set up registration societies aimed at drawing voters into their group. Over the years these societies grew into social clubs, with members voting according to whichever one they belonged to. The two parties began to produce manifestos – written summaries of the policies they wanted to bring into government.

A nineteenth-century illustration of the House of Commons. The Speaker sits in the centre at the far end. In the foreground stands the young William Ewart Gladstone, recently elected to Parliament as Conservative MP for Newark.

By the beginning of the twentieth century, British politics was presided over by a two-party system of Liberals and Tories. In 1918 the right to vote was extended to all men over the age of 21 and women over the age of 30, tripling the electorate. In 1928 that right was extended to all women over the age of 21. As the century progressed, support for the Liberals dwindled, and the Labour Party became one of the two major parties in Britain.

How the two-party system works

Since 1945, the UK has mainly been governed either by the Labour Party or by the Conservative Party. The two parties together have taken between 75 per cent and 97 per cent of the vote in general elections and have always put forward parliamentary candidates in every constituency.

Some people have described the UK electoral system as a two-and-a-half party system, with the Liberal Democrats forming the third group, and contesting nearly all the seats. Since the early 1980s, nationalist movements in Scotland, Northern Ireland and Wales have resulted in the election to Parliament of MPs representing the interests of these countries. These MPs are members of nationalist parties, rather than members of the two main parties. Following the 2001 general election, there were thirteen different parties represented in the House of Commons.

The rise of the Labour Party
As the electorate grew, working-class people began to be frustrated by what they saw as a lack of representation in Parliament. Although the Liberal Party championed social reform, it was not prepared to put forward candidates from working-class organizations such as trade unions. In 1868, a national congress of trade unions was formed. It was followed by the foundation of the Labour Party in 1906. In 1918, both organizations began to put forward their own candidates. Their proposed policies included full employment, a minimum wage, maximum working hours, public ownership of industry, taxation of wealthy people at a higher rate than the poor, and the expansion of social services. As working-class men and women were now able to vote, these policies became very popular. By 1922 the Labour Party had more MPs than the Liberal Party and had become the official opposition party to the Conservative government. In 1924, the Labour Party briefly formed the government in coalition with the Liberal Party.

The two-party system

Strengths
- it provides stable, strong governments that don't have to keep calling general elections. In multi-party systems or in proportional representation systems, there are frequent elections.
- it means that governments can keep their election promises and policies are stable over long periods.
- it keeps people interested in what their government is doing, as the two parties fight it out in the media for the support of the electorate.

Weaknesses
- it doesn't really represent the way in which UK citizens vote. The degree of support for the smaller parties is not represented in Parliament.
- governments do not need to find a consensus when they make their policies, instead they rely on their strong majorities in Parliament to push laws through.
- it could be seen as time-wasting, reducing politics to a team game with the emphasis on personality rather than issues. This may result in voter apathy, with people growing increasingly fed-up with the sight of the two main parties endlessly squaring up for a fight.

At Prime Minister's Questions, Tony Blair (standing) faces Opposition MPs over the despatch box in the House of Commons.

Although other parties have seats in the Commons, the idea that there is largely a two-party system is still supported by the media. Television debates and news reports aim to offer a balance of ideas, rather than appear to favour one party over another. This often results in politics being presented as a competition between two opposing parties. Television companies compete with one another for viewers, so they like to present political debates as exciting events. The two major parties encourage this approach because it works in their interest, and they are usually willing to provide the media with a government and Opposition spokesperson who, naturally, present conflicting ideas.

Devolution

After the elections of 1997, new national assemblies were created for Northern Ireland, Scotland and Wales in a process called devolution. The creation of these separate parliaments has affected the two-party system. While there was only one Parliament – in Westminster – parties that wanted to effect political change in Wales, Scotland or Northern Ireland could only try to do so there. Sometimes the government would be influenced by nationalists' demands because it depended on their vote. Towards the end of the 1992-1997 Parliament, the Conservative government's overall majority fell to five. This meant that it needed to seek support from the minority parties – in this case, the Northern Ireland Unionist parties – to be certain of passing the laws it wanted. Many people have suggested that, during this period, the government's policies on Northern Ireland were influenced by this dependence. The creation of the national assemblies has removed many of the issues concerning the UK's regions from Westminster.

A polling station in Stirling, Scotland, in 1997. The voting was for a referendum on the issue of devolution. The outcome was a resounding majority in favour of self-government.

How Political Parties are Managed

The House of Commons has 659 MPs. In 2002, all except one of these were members of UK political parties. The political party that has been elected to govern produces a series of planned bills. These bills are based on the ideas outlined in the party's election manifesto, which the party in government hopes to turn into law. If the governing party has a large, loyal majority who will vote for it, a bill's passage through the Commons is guaranteed. However, if the governing party has a small majority, then it may lose the vote.

The House of Commons is designed for the two-party system, with the two main parties sitting opposite one another (the Liberal Democrats also occupy the Opposition benches). In the last two parliaments this has caused a seating problem, with not enough seats on one side of the House and a surplus on the other. For example, in the 2002 Parliament, almost twice as many MPs were sitting on the government side of the Commons chamber as on the Opposition benches.

The illustration below shows the layout of the House of Commons. The government and the Opposition face one another across the floor of the House.

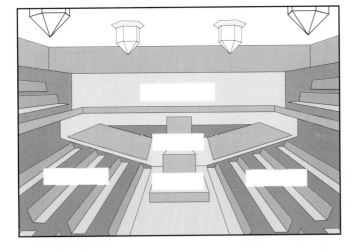

Parliamentary meetings

After the 2001 election, the Labour Party had 413 MPs, the Conservatives had 166 and the Liberal Democrats had 52. The parties hold parliamentary party meetings, attended by backbenchers (MPs with no government post) and by ministers (if the party is in power) or shadow ministers (if the party is in opposition). For the party in power, these meetings allow backbench MPs to put their ideas forward and, if necessary, criticize their party's policies in a way that wouldn't be tolerated in the Commons. The parties in Parliament also hold committees to discuss certain issues and so influence party policy in that way.

Conservative leader, Iain Duncan Smith leads his first party conference in October 2001.

Parties and policies

When parties decide on their policies they have to find a compromise between their beliefs, their desire to attract voters and the ideals of their party activists. In the past, Conservative Party policies were decided by the leadership and presented to the party members at the annual conference, having taken into account the feelings of party members. The Labour Party, on the other hand, had usually developed policies at local party and trade union level.

A school science lesson. Standards in education and school class sizes tend to be fiercely debated topics between the parties at election time.

Local government and the party system

Political parties not only have groups of MPs in national government – councillors in local government also tend to belong to political parties. Voters at local elections are influenced both by national issues and local issues. Between 1974 and the 1990s, the number of Liberal Democrat local councillors increased by 400 per cent. This resulted in many 'hung' councils, in other words councils in which there was no overall majority. Hung councils often lead to coalition local governments where two parties, usually Labour or Conservative plus the Liberal Democrats, agree to vote together. Many people see this as a good thing because it forces council members to negotiate a compromise. These hung councils better represent the voters' wishes, because more than one party can have an influence on policies.

However, other people believe that hung councils are a waste of time, because every issue has to be negotiated and no single, clear policy is followed. In local councils where one party dominates, policy decisions are often taken before the council meetings. As only a small number of people bother to vote in local elections this can mean that people with a very small mandate (degree of support) are running the local services, such as schools and hospitals.

Changes in structure and beliefs

In more recent times, this way of developing policies has changed for both major parties. Labour used to debate and decide on its policies by vote at the Labour Party conference. After a series of election defeats in the 1980s and 1990s, the Labour Party made changes in its internal structure, reducing the power of the trade unions to decide policy and the power of local activists to decide who parliamentary candidates should be. Labour Party conferences, which were once highly charged debates where policy decisions were voted on, became more streamlined. They are now more of a showcase for party values than a decision-making forum. The Conservative Party has become more democratic. Party members now have a greater say in policy making, and disputes about policy – particularly regarding the European Union – are aired more openly.

The way in which policies are aimed at the electorate has also changed. In the past, the Labour Party was supported largely by the working class, and its policies were designed to attract working-class votes. The Conservative Party was the party of business, property and wealth and its voters tended to be middle-class, home-owning people. These social divisions have altered during the past twenty years. Now many more people own homes, fewer are employed in manual work, and not many appear to be interested in party politics.

The policies and political beliefs of the parties have changed to accommodate these factors. Both Conservative and Labour parties have moved towards the centre ground of politics. The Labour Party has abandoned its commitment to public ownership and portrays itself as the party of

Arthur Scargill, then leader of the National Union of Mineworkers, receives a standing ovation at the Labour Party conference in 1984. In recent years, having decided that its link with the unions was not generally popular, the Labour Party has made efforts to distance itself from them.

business. The Conservative Party is also in a state of change but has not yet found a way to portray itself as an effective government. For many people, this move by both parties into the middle ground suggests that they are no longer true to their political beliefs. Both parties use focus groups (randomly selected groups of people) and opinion polls to find out what the voters want before they decide what their policies will be.

Political parties and their finances

Political parties spend large amounts of money, particularly at election times. In 2001 the Conservative Party spent £12.77 million on its election campaign, while the Labour Party spent £11.14 million and the Liberal Democrats £1.36 million. In addition to the costs of elections, there is the day-to-day running of the party machinery.

This Conservative Party candidate makes clear his opposition to a single European currency.

Donations In the 1980s and 1990s, there was a great deal of publicity about where the parties found their funds. There were claims in the press that in some cases funds came from foreign businesses, or were the result of promises of public honours, such as a knighthood or an OBE, and influence with government.

Traditionally, funding for both parties has come from party membership fees, levied on individual members. Also, in the period following the Second World War, the Conservative Party received 60 per cent of its funds in donations from businesses, and the Labour Party received 80 per cent of its funds in donations from the trade unions. Since the 1970s this arrangement has changed dramatically, with business donations to the Conservatives falling to 20 per cent and trade union donations to Labour falling to 35 per cent. Both parties now rely much more on donations from wealthy individuals.

During the 1997 general election campaign, celebrities such a Eddie Izzard (above right) made substantial donat to the Labour Party.

Leader of the Liberal Democrats, Charles Kennedy (centre, with microphone) on the campaign trail in June 2001.

After the 1997 general election, the new Labour government set up a committee to look into party financing and make recommendations on improving it. In 1998 the Neill Committee recommended the disclosure of sources for donations of more than £5,000. It also suggested banning foreign companies or individuals from donating to UK political parties, a ban on anonymous donations, and a limit of £30,000 per constituency (a total of £19.25 million nationally) on election campaigns. It recommended that companies wishing to donate to political parties should first ballot their shareholders and get their permission. The only company to have done so in the past received a vote of 80 per cent against making political contributions!

Election campaigns

Elections for Parliament (general elections) take place in the UK at least once every five years. Elections for local government and the parliament of the European Union take place at fixed intervals of four and five years respectively. The Prime Minister decides exactly when the next general election will be, usually at a time when the government seems to be doing well in the opinion polls.

Long before an election is called, the parties plan and print their manifestos and politicians begin their pre-election campaigning. Over the years, election campaigning has changed from a chiefly local activity, with candidates travelling around their constituencies, to a national event, with candidates focusing their attention chiefly on television, radio and national newspaper coverage.

'This deal will only serve to fuel the anti-globalization protesters who are already threatening to barricade the conference. I would rather be outside the conference associated with them, than inside having anything to do with McDonald's.' John Cryer, a backbench Labour Party MP, speaking about the McDonald's burger chain sponsorship of a reception at the Labour Party conference. In August 2001 it was revealed that the Labour Party had accepted sponsorship from McDonald's, a company that has been criticized by environmental protestors.

YOU PAID THE TAX

So where are the trains?

Conservatives
www.conservatives.com

Advertising National elections are organized by teams of professionals working at party headquarters and involve the services of advertising agencies, which can be paid millions of pounds for devising advertising campaigns. Voters are targeted via computer technology, which can identify certain social groups. Those targeted include people who work in a particular industry, or groups with lifestyles in common – for example, pensioners, divorcées, and single parents. Canvassers spend the weeks in the run up to the election telephoning individuals to obtain feedback and persuading them to vote for a particular party. On the streets, huge posters portray the leaders of each of the political parties. Each party with 50 or more candidates is allowed free air-time on television to make its election broadcasts.

At the local level the party machinery still moves into action. Candidates are given free use of the postal system, leaflets and posters are printed and candidates or their representatives visit as many houses as they can, hoping to persuade electors to vote for them.

A Conservative Party election poster criticizes the Labour government's performance with regard to the UK's national rail network.

Marginal seats Not all constituencies

receive an equal amount of attention from the parties. Marginal seats (where two parties have in the past polled a similar number of votes) are honoured with high profile visits from the party leaders. Other target areas include constituencies in which there are floating voters – people who have no long-term commitment to any one party. In the period leading up to the 1997 general election, the Labour Party significantly changed its image with voters. It shifted its target voter to 'middle England votes' – people such as upwardly mobile, working-class people from the south-east of England and the middle classes of the Midlands – both groups that had voted Conservative in previous elections. In the 2001 election, a much more confident Labour Party still targeted this group.

The 1997 and 2001 election manifestos focused on a small number of issues. These shortened manifestos are called 'contracts'. They may simplify the issues for the voters, but their existence puts extra pressure on the winning party to make good its election promises.

Visits by prominent MPs to key marginals at election time provide political parties with vital photo opportunities.

The number of people joining political parties in the UK has been falling since the 1950s. It is estimated that there are about 330,000 members of the Conservative Party, 390,000 members of the Labour Party and 90,000 members of the Liberal Democrat Party. Far fewer people still are active party members. Very small numbers go to party meetings, donate to party funds beyond their membership fees, hand out leaflets at election times or canvass voters. The average age of a member of the Conservative Party is 62 years, while the average age of Labour Party members is 48 years.

Party activists have many different roles, as MPs or members of the government, as local councillors, or just as keen supporters of the local party. They choose the candidates for national and local elections, campaign on behalf of the party, raise funds, and have a much more significant effect on the policies of their party than the rest of the electorate.

A party activist outside a polling station gathers information about the choices that voters made on election day.

How parties select their leaders

The main parties have different ways of choosing their leaders. The leader and deputy leader of the Labour Party are chosen by a group made up of the trade unions, Labour MPs and the local Labour parties. Once the leader is elected, he or she chooses the people who will make up his or her Cabinet (or Shadow Cabinet) and hold office when the party is in government. The Conservative Party chooses its leader by a vote of the parliamentary party and then allows a vote of the entire membership of the party. The Conservative leader, once elected, also chooses his or her Cabinet/Shadow Cabinet colleagues and government ministers from among Conservative MPs.

A selection of campaign leaflets from the 2001 general election. Party activists play an important role in distributing such leaflets.

Tactical voting

In the 2001 general election, the voters of three constituencies in Dorset voted tactically. In one, where the Liberal Democrats had no chance of winning, some people who would normally have voted Liberal Democrat voted for Labour. In another constituency, where Labour had no chance of winning, some people who would usually have voted Labour voted for the Liberal Democrats. The activity was organized on a web site set up by left-wing musician, Billy Bragg. After the event he had this to say: 'The web site was a catalyst and a hook for focusing the debate in Dorset. What the internet offers is a form of constant protest that doesn't rely on people getting together — it's 'accessible activism'. It brought activists you wouldn't normally meet out of the woodwork to support tactical voting, which is particularly important for somewhere like Dorset that has a low political profile. The internet broadens the debate and allows people to interact. Our campaign and our web site didn't defeat the Tory candidate in South Dorset but they facilitated it, which is what democracy is all about.'

Party approval The local parties select parliamentary candidates. The Labour candidates are chosen from a list put forward by the Labour Party National Executive Committee (NEC) and from other nominees, such as trade unions. The local party chooses a shortlist from all the nominations, which it interviews and votes on. The chosen candidate then has to be approved by the NEC. Sometimes the NEC intervenes and imposes its own candidate on the constituency. The NEC also imposes a minimum number of women candidates, which differs from one constituency to another. It is considering reintroducing women-only shortlists to increase the number of women MPs at Westminster.

The Conservative local parties select their own candidates from an approved list of about 800 nominees chosen by the Conservative Party Central Office. Anyone on the list can apply to any local party for the job.

At local government level, a team of councillors is chosen by each of the local parties and voters usually vote for the whole team. Local councillors are unpaid, only claiming for expenses, and hold other full-time jobs or are retired.

Parties and government After it has been elected to government, about one third of the parliamentary party is offered government jobs. The rest of the parliamentary party may be relatively inexperienced MPs who hope one day to secure a government post. Those with jobs are careful to obey the party rules, partly because they believe in them and partly because they want to keep their jobs. Those without jobs know that if they perform well they may be rewarded with a good position in the government. Other incentives to comply include

There are many small political groups who have little hope of influencing government policy. Like this representative of the Socialist Party, a small left-wing organization, members take their campaigning on to the streets.

the offer of a place on an important parliamentary committee, perhaps studying government bills or investigating a government department.

Occasionally MPs become unhappy with their party's policies and vote against the party or ask difficult questions in Parliament. When the Conservatives were in power during the 1990s, a group of backbench MPs regularly voted against the government on the issue of Europe. Their actions resulted in the defeat of the government three times in the House of Commons.

Within the parliamentary parties there are factions, or sub-groups of the parties with a common viewpoint. In the Labour Party there is the Campaign group, 30 MPs who oppose the drift of party values towards what they believe to be right-wing politics. Other groups include the New Left in New Labour, which is opposed to the centralization of power. Within the Conservative Party there are Eurosceptic and Europhile (anti and pro European) groups as well as groups which favour stronger immigration controls, more privatization of industry, and social reform.

Toeing the line
Occasionally even a senior Cabinet member feels that they have to speak out against some issue of government policy. One person who has done this while still maintaining her Cabinet post is the Minister for Overseas Development, Clare Short. Since taking her post in 1997 she has criticized government policy and her colleagues several times, most recently over the war in Afghanistan in 2001, about which she said: 'Military action is only a small part of the strategy. At times like this the media and a lot of men go mad. It's all those toys they played with when they were children. But there are broader principles in place relating to our limited objectives in Afghanistan and the humanitarian effort.'

Clare Short speaking her mind at a press conference on the war in Afghanistan.

You and Political Parties

You have probably come into contact with political parties at election times when your school was closed and television programming was dominated by party political broadcasts and discussion shows. Sometimes politics can be quite exciting. In 2001, you may have watched the Deputy Prime Minister get into a physical fight with a heckler after an egg-throwing episode. Even when there is not an election in the offing, there are scheduled television programmes where representatives of government, Opposition and the Liberal Democrats appear regularly to discuss issues of the day.

At the age of eighteen, you are registered to vote and can make your own decision about which party is best suited to rule the country in a way that meets your needs and values. When this happens you should be aware of the choices open to you.

Young people exercising their right to vote in an election for the first time.

Voter apathy So why should you go to the trouble of voting? Your vote is unlikely to swing the result of the election in a safe seat. In a marginal seat your vote might make a difference, but now that the political parties have all moved closer together in their policies what is there to choose between them? In the 2001 general election, many people must have felt this way because the turnout at the polling stations was the lowest ever recorded. Only 60 per cent of the people who were entitled to vote bothered to do so.

Some countries make voting at election time compulsory. Do you think we should do this in the UK? In the past, many people in the UK campaigned and fought for the right to vote.

Right: a ballot paper is slipped into a sealed ballot box. When polling closes, the box will be taken to a centre, opened, and the ballots sorted and counted.

Some people even died fighting for it. In countries such as South Africa, many people were denied their democratic voting rights for generations. In such countries, people value their right to vote very highly. Because of voter apathy, a government could come to power that people dislike intensely. If such a situation should arise, then surely the voters cannot complain?

Activity
Try running an election campaign in your school.

1. Select candidates to represent each of the national parties, and just for fun, some of the other parties that also stand, such as the Monster Raving Loony Party. Provide each of them with a campaign team to research the policies of their party. Each group should find out what its party's policies are on issues such as selection in schools, welfare benefits, working mothers, the Euro, the environment, how to pay for pensions and hospitals, and asylum seekers. You could do this by contacting the local constituency party, reading the newspapers, writing to your MP, or checking the internet for information.

2. Each group should draw up an election manifesto of about five points. You should then advertise this – perhaps on noticeboards, by getting permission to go into classes and make a speech, or by conducting interviews in the school. Try to focus on issues that will affect your electorate, such as education, street crime, or curfews for teenagers. Class teachers could arrange a 'Question Time', where the selected candidates could answer questions from an audience.

3. Choose a day when the voting will take place and conduct your secret ballot. Have fun!

Glossary

anti-sleaze platform a policy of getting rid of corruption or cheating among MPs

bill a proposed law which has been put before Parliament

canvassers people who telephone or visit houses to ask people what their opinions are on an issue

coalition a group of two political parties who agree to govern together

consensus agreement

constituency an area of the country whose votes elect an MP

devolution transferring substantial powers from central government to local or regional authorities

electioneering going about the country talking to people and making speeches about the forthcoming election

electorate the people who are allowed to vote in a general election

Europhile someone who supports the idea of closer connections with the European Union, such as a single currency and the same taxation system for every country

Eurosceptic someone who is opposed to a closer union with the European Union

free market an economy where the running of business is not altered or interfered with by the government

full employment a situation in which all those people who need work have jobs

local council member someone who has been elected to sit on the council of a town or local government area and who decides on matters of local policy and spending

mandate the agreement of the people who elect a person to do a job

manifesto a written document prepared by a political party which explains its plans for when it gets into government

manual work work chiefly done with the hands and involving largely physical activity

minimum wage the least amount that can legally be paid to someone for doing a job

minister an important member of the government, in charge of an area of policy

multi-party systems political systems in which there are more than two main parties

nationalist someone whose political ideas are dominated by the interests of their country

opinion poll a survey that tries to discover what people think about an issue

party activist someone who takes an interest in the business of one particular political party

party official a party representative

patronage giving out favours or jobs to people

polling station the place at which voters register their votes at election time

right-wing used to describe ideas or people who are very conservative in nature

safe seat a constituency in which a large majority of people always vote for the same party

seats places allocated in the House of Commons for MPs

shadow ministers a group of Opposition MPs who have been given the job of taking over as ministers if they win the next election

social reform changes to the social structure of a country

social services a state-run organization that looks after the well-being of citizens

state ownership of industry a type of economy where the government owns the businesses and factories

tabloid press the most widely bought newspapers with a high content of show business and celebrity news with large head-lines and photographs. Tabloid refers to the newspapers' shape – half the size of the more 'serious' broadsheet newspapers.

trade unions an organization that represents the interests of workers in a particular industry

upwardly-mobile moving up the social ladder, earning more money

voter apathy a condition said to affect people who are eligible to vote but are not interested in voting

Resources

Information books

Andrew Marr, *Ruling Britannia*, Michael Joseph, 1995

Coxall and Robins, *Contemporary British Politics*, Macmillan, 1998

Stephen Ingle, *The British Party System*, Pinter, 2000

Tony Wright ed., *The British Political Process*, Routledge, 2000

Citizenship for All, The Citizenship Foundation, Nelson Thornes, 1998

Nigel Smith, *Great Buildings: Houses of Parliament*, Hodder Wayland, 1997

Sean Connolly et al., *Heinemann Profiles: Margaret Thatcher*, Heinemann, 2001

Andrew Langley et al., *Modern Britain*, Heinemann, 1994

The internet

http://www.labour.org.uk/
the official web site of the Labour Party

http://www.guardian.co.uk/labour/
a collection of articles about the Labour Party in the *Guardian* newspaper. Similar collections can be found by replacing 'labour' with the names of the other parties.

http://www.conservatives.com/
the web site of the Conservative Party

http://www.libdems.org.uk/
the web site of the Liberal Democrat Party. Links to local organizations.

http://www.proeuro.co.uk/
the web site of the group of Conservatives committed to the European Union

http://www.observer.co.uk/
a collection of articles on the parties

http://www.greenparty.org.uk/
the official web site of the Green Party

http://www.omrlp.com
the web site of the Monster Raving Loony Party

Index

Numbers in **bold** refer to illustrations.

backbenchers 16, 21, 27
ballot paper **7**
Bell, Martin 5
bills 15, 27
Blair, Tony **5**, **13**, **23**
Bragg, Billy 25

Cabinet, the 4, 5, **5**, 24, 27
Campaign group 27
canvassers 22
Conservative Party 8-9, 11, 12, 16, 17, 18-19, **19**, 20, 24, 27
    Central Office 26
constituencies 4, 9, 12, 21, 23, 25, 26

Democratic Unionist Party 9
devolution 9, 14, **14**
Duncan Smith, Iain **16**

education 8, **17**
election broadcasts 22
election campaigns 6, 21, 22, 29
electioneering 6, 10
elections
    bye **4**
    general 4, 5, 7, **8**, 9, 12, 13, 14, 16, 19, 21, 23, 25, 28
    local 17, 21
electoral reform 10-12
electorate 6, 10, 12, 13, 24
environmental protection 9
European Union 18, 21
Europhiles 27
Eurosceptics 27

first-past-the-post 9
floating voters 23
focus groups 19

Gladstone, William Ewart **11**

governing party 4, 7, 15
government 4, 5, 6, 7, 9, 13, **15**, 20, 21, 24, 26-7
Green Party 6, 9, **9**

Hamilton, Neil 5
House of Commons 4, **11**, 12, **13**, 14, 15, 16, 27
hung councils 17

Independent MPs 5
Izzard, Eddie **20**

Kennedy, Charles **20**

Labour Party 4, **7**, 8-9, 12, 16, 17, 18, 19, 20, 23, 24, 25, 27
    National Executive Committee (NEC) 26
Liberal Democrat Party 8-9, 12, 15, 16, 17, 19, **20**, 24, 25, 28
Liberal Party 4, 11, 12
local government 17

manifestos 6, **7**, 11, 15, 21, 23
marginal seats 23, **23**, 28
ministers 16

National Health Service (NHS) 7, 8
Neill Committee 21
New Left 27
Northern Ireland 14

opinion polls 19, 21
Opposition, the 5, 7, **13**, 14, 15, **15**
overall majority 4, 5, 14, 17

Parliament 4, 5, 6, 7, 10, 12, 13, 14, 15, 16, 21, 27
    Members of 4, 5, 6, 9, 10, 12, 15, 16, 17, 24, 26, 27
parliamentary democracy 5

party
    activists 16, 18, 24, **24**, 25
    conference 16, **16**, 18, **18**, 21
    funding 20-21
    leaders **16**, 23, 24
    membership 20, 24
    officials 6
Plaid Cymru 9
police 7
policies 6, 7, 11, 12, 13, 16, 17, 18, 19, 24, 27
politicians 6
Prime Minister 4, 5, **5**, **13**, 21
privatization 8
Progressive Unionist Party 9
proportional representation 9, 12
public services 7
public spending 8

Reform Act, 1832 10
rotten boroughs 10

Scargill, Arthur **18**
Scottish National Party (SNP) 9
Short, Clare 27, **27**
single European currency 5, **19**
Sinn Fein 9
Social Democratic and Labour Party (SDLP) 9

tactical voting 25
taxation 8, 12
trade unions 12, 16, 18, 20, 24, 26

Ulster Unionists 9

voter apathy 13, 28-9
voters 6, **6**, 8, 10-11, 16, 17, 18, 19, 22, 23, 25, 26
voting systems 9